LITTLE
JOHNNY

SARCASM & WIT
A COLLECTION OF LITTLE JOHNNY JOKES

John Laird

iUniverse, Inc.
New York   Bloomington

iUniverse books may be ordered through booksellers or by contacting:

iUniverse
1663 Liberty Drive
Bloomington, IN 47403
www.iuniverse.com
1-800-Authors (1-800-288-4677)

ISBN: 978-1-4401-2541-6 (sc)
ISBN: 978-1-4401-2539-3 (ebook)

Printed in the United States of America

iUniverse rev. date: 02/26/2009

LITTLE
JOHNNY

M&M'S...

Little Johnny and Lanie decide to go trick-or-treating dressed up like M&M's. After ringing the first doorbell of the night, an elderly couple greets them, "Why, both of you are just too cute. What exactly are you supposed to be?"

Little Johnny answers, "We're M&M's...She's plain...and I've got nuts."

THREE LITTLE PIGS...

Following recess one afternoon, Miss Jones decides to read her class the story of the Three Little Pigs.

Following a brief introduction, Miss Jones continues, "The first little pig approaches a gentleman selling straw and says, 'Pardon me sir, I would like to purchase some of your straw to build a house with.' Now class, what do you think the gentleman's reply is?" asks Miss Jones.

"Holy crap...a talking pig!" hollers Little Johnny.

INSERT FOOT HERE...

To earn a little extra spending money one summer, Little Johnny accepts a part-time job at Old Man Taylor's store. One of Little Johnny's first customers is a gentleman who wants to buy half a head of lettuce. Little Johnny patiently explains to the customer that such a purchase requires Old Man Taylor's approval. Little

Johnny excuses himself, but ensures the customer that he will return as soon as possible with the required approval.

As he enters Old Man Taylor's office Little Johnny hollers, "There's some jerk-off out here wantin' to buy half a head of lettuce…" Before he can even get the complete sentence out of his mouth Little Johnny notices out of the corner of his eye that the customer is now standing directly beside him, so without hesitation Little Johnny continues, "…And this fine gentleman would like to buy the other half!"

Old Man Taylor quickly approves the sale and the satisfied customer leaves the store. Before Little Johnny can mutter a word, Old Man Taylor smiles wryly at the boy and says, "I'm quite impressed with the way you handled yourself just now…you think quick on your feet. Are you from around here?"

"I'm originally from Canada, sir," replies Little Johnny.

"Oh really? How'd you like living in Canada?"

"Ain't nothin' in Canada but whores and hockey players."

"My wife is from Canada."

"Oh yeah, what team did she play for?"

WHERE DO BABIES COME FROM?

After overhearing some rather confusing adult conversation recently, Little Johnny innocently asks, "Mommy, where do babies come from?"

His mother replies, "The stork brings them."

"Then who screws the stork?"

WATERING HOLE...

Little Johnny is visiting his aunt and uncle's farm one weekend, when his Aunt J.J. asks him to head down to the watering hole and get her some water to cook dinner with. Before he could even dip the bucket underneath the water, Little Johnny saw two menacing eyes staring up at him. So he immediately dropped the bucket and high-tailed it back to the farmhouse.

"Well now, where's my bucket and where's my water?" Aunt J.J. asks him.

"I can't get water from there," exclaims Johnny. "There's a big ol' gator down there!"

"Don't mind that ol' gator. Why, he's probably as scared of you, as you are of him."

"Well, if he's as scared of me, as I am of him, then that water ain't fit to drink!"

WISHFUL THINKING…

One hot summer day, Old Man Taylor is sitting on his front porch, reading the newspaper and drinking a cold beer, when Little Johnny comes walking down the road carrying a big bundle of wire.

"Hey kid!" the old man says, "Where you going with that wire?"

"Well," Little Johnny says, "this here ain't just wire, this here's chicken wire…I'm fixin' to catch me some chickens."

"You can't catch chickens with chicken wire!"

"Sure I can!" Little Johnny explains as he takes off down the road. At the end of the day, sure enough, he's got a whole mess of chickens caught in this chicken wire.

Well, Old Man Taylor is sitting on his porch the next day, and Little Johnny comes walking down the road, carrying a big roll of tape.

"Hey kid! Where you going with that tape?"

"Well, this here ain't just tape, this here's duck tape…I'm fixin' to catch me some ducks."

"You can't catch ducks with duck tape!"

"Sure I can!" Little Johnny explains as he takes off down the road. Toward the end of the day, the old man can't believe his eyes. The kid has a whole bunch of ducks all wrapped up tight in this tape of his.

The next day Old Man Taylor is sitting on his porch again, and Little Johnny comes walking down the road carrying what looks like a handful of weeds.

"Hey kid! Where you going with those weeds?"

"Well, this here ain't just weeds, this here's pussy willow."

"Hang on," the old man says. "I'll get my hat!"

UNDER THE WEATHER...

Little Johnny's parents decide to have him circumcised. After a few days of recovery, Little Johnny returns to school. An hour or so after homeroom, the pain is really starting to bother him and he asks Miss Jones if he can go see the school nurse. Seeing that Little Johnny is in obvious pain, she allows him to go.

Immediately, the nurse suggests that Little Johnny call his mother to see if she will come and get him. The nurse politely waits in the other room while he makes the call. A few minutes pass, and Little Johnny exits the room and starts walking back to class. The nurse can't help but notice that Little Johnny's penis is hanging out of his trousers.

Obviously concerned, the nurse asks, "Little Johnny, what are you doing? You can't walk around like that!"

"Well," he replies, "I told my Mommy how much it hurt and she said if I could just stick it out 'til lunch time...she'd pick me up then."

FASCINATE...

Miss Jones asks her students to use the word fascinate in a sentence.

Stephanie says, "My family's trip to the Grand Canyon last summer was fascinating."

"That's not bad Stephanie," explains Miss Jones. "But I was hoping you would use the word fascinate."

Tim raises his hand and says, "I was fascinated by the magician that performed at my birthday party."

"Not bad." says Miss Jones, "But can anyone use the word fascinate in its present tense?"

Little Johnny stands up and says, "My sis has a sweater with ten buttons, but her tits are so big she can only fasten eight!"

TIMBUKTU ...

One morning Miss Jones asks for two volunteers to participate in a poetry contest. The rules are simple; compose a four-line poem containing the word Timbuktu.

The first volunteer is Joey, an instant favorite to win this contest... straight-A's, class president and overall do-gooder. After a few moments thought, Joey begins his poem:

> "Slowly across the desert sand
> Trekked a dusty caravan
> Men on camels...two by two
> Destination...Timbuktu."

The class is indeed impressed and none of them seem to be able to muster up enough courage to challenge Joey's impromptu gem...none of them except Little Johnny, who immediately selects himself as the final volunteer. Without hesitation, Little Johnny clears his throat and begins his poem:

> "Tim and me...a huntin' we went
> Met three whores in a pop-up tent
> They was three...we was two
> So I bucked one and Timbuktu."

THINK OUTSIDE THE BOX...

It is Miss Jones' birthday and her students are gathered around her desk waiting on their turn to present her with a gift.

Well, Missy's father owns a small florist shop, so when she presents her gift, Miss Jones shakes it and says, "I'll bet I know what it is... some flowers."

"But how did you know?" asks Missy.

"Oh, just a wild guess."

Well, Mike's parents own a candy store in the mall so when he presents his gift, Miss Jones shakes it and says, "I'll bet I know what it is...a box of candy."

"But how did you know?" asks Mike.

"Oh, just a wild guess."

It is now Little Johnny's turn. As Miss Jones shakes his gift she notices that it is leaking. Well, considering Little Johnny's father owns the local liquor store, Miss Jones says, "I'll bet I know what it is...a bottle of wine."

"Nope!"

Somewhat curious by now, Miss Jones uses her finger to taste the leakage and asks, "Is it champagne?"

"Nope!"

Once again she tastes the leakage and confesses, "I give up...what is it?"

"A puppy!"

ORANGES...

Miss Jones begins her math lesson, "If I have seven oranges in one hand, and I have eight oranges in the other hand, what would I have?"

"You'd have mighty big hands," answers Little Johnny.

CHANGE OF PLANS...

On the first day of school following summer vacation, Miss Jones asks the class if any of them went on a family trip.

Little Johnny starts first, "My family visited my great-grandmother in Minnesota."

Eyeing an opportunity, Miss Jones asks, "Very good. Can you tell the class how you spell Minnesota?"

"Well…we actually went to Ohio."

IS THAT TOO MUCH TO ASK?

Following his grandfather's wake, Little Johnny begins a conversation with Father Harrison, "I sure was impressed by all the kind words you said about my grandfather this evening."

Touched by this, Father Harrison asks, "Well, have you thought about what you'd like people to say about you at your wake?"

"I sure have. I'd like them to say, 'look…he's still moving!'"

CREATIVE ADDITION…

Miss Jones notices that Little Johnny once again isn't paying attention during math class. Therefore, she calls on him and asks, "Little Johnny! What are 4, 2, 28 and 44?"

Little Johnny quickly replies, "NBC, CBS, HBO and the Cartoon Network!"

HOPE…

While her class was taking its weekly spelling test, Miss Jones sternly asks, "Little Johnny, I hope I didn't just see you looking at Mike's paper!"

Little Johnny answers, "I hope you didn't either!"

SNOW ANGEL…

Little Johnny thought it would be a good idea to go outside and play in the fresh snow. Not long afterward, his mother decides to join him. She lies down on the snow and waves both her arms and legs through the snow…creating a snow angel. Wondering if her son had ever done this before she asks, "What do I look like?"

"An idiot," answers Little Johnny.

MAN OF THE HOUSE…

Little Johnny rushes home from school. He invades the fridge and is scooping out some cherry vanilla ice cream…when his mother enters the kitchen.

She says, "Put that away Little Johnny. You can't have ice cream now. It's too close to suppertime. Go outside and play."

Little Johnny whimpers and says, "There's no one to play with."

Trying to pacify him, she says, "OK. I'll play with you. What do you want to play?"

He says, "I wanna play Mommy and Daddy."

To further appease him, she says, "Fine, I'll play. What do I do?"

Little Johnny says, "Go up to the bedroom and lie down."

Figuring that she can easily control the situation...his mother goes upstairs.

Little Johnny, feeling a bit cocky, swaggers down the hall and opens the utility closet. He dons his father's old fishing hat and as he starts up the stairs, he notices a cigarette butt in the ashtray on the end table. He picks it up and slips it in the corner of his mouth.

At the top of the stairs, he moves to the bedroom doorway. His mother rises up and says, "What do I do now?"

In a gruff manner, Little Johnny says, "Get your ass downstairs and get that boy some ice cream!"

PARTNERS IN CRIME...

A stranger is walking down the sidewalk one afternoon when he notices that Little Johnny is having trouble reaching the doorbell of one the houses. Even when he jumps...he can't quite reach it. Well, the stranger decides to help the boy out. He walks up onto the porch and rings the doorbell.

He looks down at the boy, smiles and asks, "What now?"

Little Johnny answers, "We'd better run like hell!"

PETER PRINCIPLE...

As Little Johnny approaches the playground, Lanie asks him to come with her and play in the bushes. Once they are behind the bushes, she says, "Let me see your peter."

Little Johnny responds, "What's a peter?"

She explains, "Well, if you don't know what a peter is, I'm not sure I want to play with you anymore."

Little Johnny is quite disturbed the rest of the afternoon. As soon as his father comes home that evening, Little Johnny asks, "Daddy, what's a peter?"

His Dad unzips his trousers says, "Son, this is a peter... and it's a perfect peter!"

The following day while on the playground, Little Johnny asks Lanie, "Wanna come play in the bushes? I found out what a peter is." Once they are behind the bushes, Little Johnny unzips his trousers and says, "Now...this is a peter...and if it was an inch shorter it'd be a perfect peter!"

EAR...

Following the tardy bell one morning, Miss Jones asks her class to be seated...they are going to have a spelling bee. "Little Johnny," she says, "You can go first. Please spell the word ear and use it in a sentence."

Little Johnny stands up and proudly spells, "e-a-r." Then, for his sentence, Little Johnny simulates taking a big hit off a joint...then while acting as though his lungs are full of smoke he pretends to pass the joint to Miss Jones and says "eeeaarr."

DEDUCTIVE REASONING...

Miss Jones wants to teach her students about the dangers of alcohol, so she plans an experiment that involves a glass of water, a shot of whiskey, and two worms.

"Now class, observe closely," she says as she places the first worm into the glass of water. In turn, the worm moves about freely...as happy as a worm in water could be.

The second worm, she places into the shot of whiskey. It moves about for a short while, and then quickly sinks to the bottom... dead as a doornail.

"Now, what lesson can we derive from this experiment?" Miss Jones asks.

Little Johnny raises his hand and responds, "Drink whiskey and you won't get worms!"

WANNA BET...

It was Little Johnny's first day of the new school year. Before class, his father briefly discusses with Miss Jones a new habit that Little Johnny has picked up over summer vacation...gambling. He warns her that Little Johnny may very well try to gamble his lunch money if he is not watched closely. Miss Jones assures him that she will keep a close eye on Little Johnny.

Shortly after lunch that same day, Little Johnny's father phones Miss Jones and asks how things are going. "Oh, everything is fine," she says. "I think I may have even cured Little Johnny of his gambling habit."

Very curious, his father asks, "Well how did you manage to do that?"

"All morning, he insisted on betting me $10 that I had a mole on my rear," she said. "I finally agreed to the bet, took him to the teacher's lounge and showed him that I had no mole."

"Damn!" the father cries out. "He bet me fifty dollars this morning that he would see your ass before the day was over."

LOADED QUESTION...

Little Johnny's mother sends him to the market for a loaf of bread. On his way home, Little Johnny is swinging the loaf of bread in one hand and has his other hand in his pocket.

Along comes Father Harrison thinking to himself that it would be an opportune time to mention a verse from the Bible to Little Johnny. He approaches Little Johnny and says, "I see, Little Johnny, that you have the Staff of Life in one hand. What do you have in the other?"

"A loaf of bread father," replies Little Johnny.

OLDEST EXCUSE IN THE BOOK...

"Little Johnny, where's your homework?" Miss Jones asks sternly while holding out her hand.

"My dog ate it," is his solemn response.

"Little Johnny, I've been a teacher for eighteen years. Do you really expect me to believe that?"

"It's true, Miss Jones, I swear!" insists Little Johnny. "I had to force him...but he ate it!"

SWEET REVENGE...

Little Johnny's grandfather pulls a beer out of the cooler one humid afternoon as they both sit on the front porch. "Grandpa, can I have one of those beers?" asks Little Johnny.

"Can your dick touch your ass?" his grandfather replies.

"Well, no it can't."

"Then you're not old enough to have a beer!"

A short time later, Little Johnny's grandfather lights up a cigar. "Grandpa, can I have one of those cigars?" asks Little Johnny.

"Can your dick touch your ass?" his grandfather replies.

"Well, no it can't."

"Then you're not old enough to smoke a cigar!"

Later that afternoon, Little Johnny strolls out of the house with two freshly baked cookies. "Do you think I could have one of those cookies?" asks the grandfather.

"Can your dick touch your ass?" Little Johnny replies.

"Well, hell yeah my dick can touch my ass!"

"Then go screw yourself…grandma made these cookies for me!"

RIGHT UNDER THEIR NOSE…

Little Johnny's class takes a field trip to their local police station where they are shown a bulletin board of the ten most wanted criminals in the country. Little Johnny points to a particular picture and asks if the man photographed is really an outlaw.

"Yes," says Sheriff Robertson, "we are searching for him desperately."

"So," Little Johnny asks, "why the hell didn't you keep him when you took his picture?"

THEY GROW UP SO FAST…

One afternoon, Little Johnny and Lanie explain to their parents that they have decided to get married.

Thinking this is cute, Lanie's Dad asks, "Where will you live?"

"Well," says Little Johnny, "I figured we could just share Lanie's room. It's plenty big for both of us."

"And how will you live?" her Dad asks.

"Together, our weekly allowances total almost $10. That should be more than enough," explains Little Johnny.

Little Johnny seems to have all the answers. However, Lanie's Dad is determined to play along…"And what if a little one comes along?"

"Well," says Little Johnny, "we've been lucky so far."

LEADING THE WITNESS…

Little Johnny misses his final exam due to the flu. Therefore, Miss Jones suggests to Principal Woodrow that they both give him an oral exam to make up for the test he's missed. Principal Woodrow agrees.

Miss Jones begins, "Little Johnny, what does a cow have four of, that I only have two of?"

"Legs," Little Johnny replies.

The next question, "Little Johnny, what do you have in your pants that I don't have in mine?"

"Pockets," he replies.

Impressed so far, Miss Jones asks, "Little Johnny, what is the capital of Italy?"

Little Johnny replies, "Rome."

Miss Jones turns to Principal Woodrow and asks, "Should we pass him?"

Principal Woodrow answers, "Don't ask me, I got the first two wrong!"

IMPATIENCE IS A VIRTUE…

Little Johnny was becoming restless as Father Harrison's sermon dragged on and on. Finally, he leaned over to his mother and whispers, "Mommy, if we go ahead and give him the money now, will he let us go?"

CHEERIOS…

The morning after spending the night with his friend Jarrod, Little Johnny decides he's tired of being treated like a child, "Hey Jarrod, when we go downstairs for breakfast, we should cuss like we're adults…you say hell and I'll say ass." Jarrod agrees and they head downstairs.

Jarrod's mother joins them in the kitchen and first asks her son what he'd like for breakfast. "Awe, hell Mom…I'll have some Cheerios!" Jarrod answers.

Whack! Jarrod flies out of his chair as his Mom backhands him… he stumbles across the kitchen floor and heads upstairs crying.

Jarrod's Mom looks at Little Johnny and says with a stern voice, "And what do you want for breakfast, young man?"

"I'm not sure," Little Johnny whimpers, "but you can bet your sweet ass it won't be Cheerios!"

POTTY TRAINING...

Following Gym class, Little Johnny and a couple of his friends were standing at the urinal.

Billy finishes up first and proceeds to wash his hands...making sure not to miss a single spot...and using at least twenty paper towels in the process. "My parents taught me to be clean."

Scotty finishes up next and heads over to the sink...proceeds to wet only the tips of his fingers and grabs a single paper towel. "My parents taught me taught me to be environmentally conscious."

As Little Johnny finishes up, he simply heads for the door and says, "My parents taught me not to piss on my hands."

DIRECT OBJECT...

Miss Jones asks Little Johnny to come up with a sentence that has a direct object.

After giving it a little thought, Little Johnny says, "Miss Jones, everyone thinks you are a strikingly beautiful woman."

"Why thank you, Little Johnny. But what is the direct object?"

"A good report card!"

TOO MUCH INFORMATION…

Little Johnny says to his mother, "Mommy, I have to tinkle."

His mother replies, "Would you like Mommy to take you?"

"No," answers Little Johnny, "let grandma . . . her hand shakes!"

THE LAST LAUGH…

The manager at Old Man Taylor's store notices that Little Johnny has been hanging out at the front of the building an awful lot lately. The manager doesn't know what Little Johnny's problem is, but the boys like to tease him. They say he is two bricks short of a load…two pickles shy of a barrel.

To prove it, sometimes the boys offer Johnny his choice between a nickel and a dime. He always takes the nickel…they say because it's bigger. One day after Little Johnny grabs the nickel, the store manager pulls him aside and asks, "Little Johnny, those boys are making fun of you. They think you don't know that a dime is worth more than a nickel. Are you grabbing the nickel because it's bigger or what?"

Little Johnny answers, "Well, if I took the dime, they would quit doing it altogether!"

GIMME...

Little Johnny and two of his buddies decide to play a round of golf. Just before teeing off, Lanie approaches the threesome and asks if she can join them...but only under one condition... that they agree not to critique her play. The boys agree, and play begins.

As they approach the eighteenth green, Lanie turns to the three boys and says, "If I sink this ten foot putt, I will have played my best round of golf ever. With that in mind, forget my comment earlier about critiquing my play. In fact, I'll plant a kiss on whichever one of you gives me the best advice toward sinking this putt."

Billy walks over, eyes the putt for a couple of seconds, and says "Lanie, aim that putt six inches to the right of the hole, and the ball will fall right into the cup."

Scotty interrupts and says, "Don't listen to him, you'll need to aim at least twelve inches to the right of the hole to make that putt."

Eyeing the situation carefully, Little Johnny confidently picks up Lanie's ball and drops it directly into the cup, "I'd say that's a gimme!"

WORD PROBLEMS...

Miss Jones calls on Little Johnny during math class one day, "If there are five birds sitting on a fence and you shoot one of them with your gun...how many birds would be left?"

"None," replies Little Johnny, "cause the rest of them would fly away."

"Well, the correct answer is four," explains Miss Jones. "But I like the way you're thinking."

"Now, I have a question for you," says Little Johnny. "If there are three ladies eating ice cream cones...one licking her cone... one biting her cone...and one sucking her cone...which lady is married?"

"Well," Miss Jones answers nervously, "I guess the one sucking her cone?"

"No," answers Little Johnny, "The one with the wedding ring on her finger. But I like the way you are thinking!"

GREETER...

While working at a fund-raising car wash one summer, Little Johnny figures that initiating small talk might yield better donations, so as the next customer approaches he says, "Good morning ma'am...your two children sure are adorable...are they twins?"

The woman rudely replies, "Hell no they're not twins, what would make you think that?"

"Well, I just find it hard to believe that you could get laid twice."

SEX EDUCATION...

Miss Jones approaches the subject of sex education with caution due to Little Johnny's propensity for sexual innuendo. To no one's surprise, Little Johnny remains attentive throughout the entire lecture. Finally, towards the end of the lesson, the teacher asks for examples of sex education from the class.

Jarrod raises his hand, "I saw a bird in her nest with some eggs."

"Very good, Jarrod," coos the teacher.

"My Mommy had a baby," says Sherry.

"Oh, that's nice," replies Miss Jones.

Finally, Little Johnny raises his hand. With much fear and trepidation, the teacher calls on him. "I was watchin' TV yesterday and I saw the Lone Ranger. He was surrounded by hundreds of Indians; they attacked all at once. In no time, the Lone Ranger killed every last one of them with only his two guns."

The teacher was relieved but puzzled, "And what does that have to do with sex education, Little Johnny?"

"It'll teach those Indians not to screw with the Lone Ranger!"

POLITICS AS USUAL...

Little Johnny comes home from school one day and asks his father, "Daddy, what can you tell me about politics? Miss Jones is gonna ask us for examples in class tomorrow."

His father thinks for a moment and answers, "OK son, the best way I can describe politics is to form an analogy. Let's pretend that I'm capitalism because I'm the breadwinner. Your mother is the government because she controls everything. Our maid represents the working class because she indeed works for us. You are the people because you answer to your mother and me. And your baby sister is the future. Does that help any?"

Little Johnny, still somewhat uncertain, answers, "Well, I don't know...I'll have to think about what you said."

Later that night, after everyone has gone to bed, Little Johnny is woken up by his baby sister's crying. Upon further investigation, he notices that his sister has a dirty diaper. So, Little Johnny strolls down the hall to his parent's room where he finds his father's side of the bed empty. His attempts to wake up his mother are unsuccessful and Little Johnny is quickly becoming discouraged. However, on the way back upstairs to his bedroom, he discovers a light on in the guest room. The room's door is slightly ajar and when he peeps through it he sees that his father is in bed with their maid. At this point, there really isn't anything he can do for his baby sister, so Little Johnny just goes back to bed.

The next morning, he says to his father at the breakfast table, "Daddy, I think I understand politics much better now."

"Excellent, my boy," he answers, "What have you learned?"

Little Johnny pauses for a moment and says, "I learned capitalism is screwing the working class...government is sound asleep and ignoring the people...and the future's full of crap!"

NON-VERBAL COMMUNICATION...

Miss Jones decides that her students should learn something about mimes, so she has each of them develop a speech, which is to be relayed by using gestures only. When Little Johnny's turn comes, he stands up in front of the class and says, "Ladies (grabbing chest) and gentlemen (grabbing crotch)...."

Miss Jones is not amused, so she sends him to the principal's office. Little Johnny explains what happened and the sympathetic principal tells him to revise his speech as follows, "Ladies (outlining a woman's curves) and gentlemen (making a muscle with his arm)...."

So Little Johnny goes back to class and proceeds to give his speech again, "Ladies (outlining a woman's curves) and gentlemen (making a muscle with his arm), it gives me great pleasure (whacking-off motion)...."

LET IT SNOW, LET IT SNOW, LET IT SNOW...

Finally back to school following an unseasonably heavy snowstorm, Miss Jones asks her students if they had used their time away from school constructively.

"I sure did," replies Little Johnny. "I prayed for more snow."

HIDDEN MEANING...

Miss Jones had given her class a homework assignment...to observe something truly exciting and relate it to the class the following day. When it came time for her students to give their reports, Miss Jones is quite reluctant to call upon Little Johnny for obvious reasons. Eventually, however, his turn did come.

Little Johnny casually walks up to the front of the classroom and with a piece of chalk, draws a small white dot on the blackboard. He then quietly sits back down.

Miss Jones is quite confused, "Little Johnny, please share with the rest of the class what that dot has to do with the assignment I gave you."

"It's a period," explains Little Johnny.

"Well, I can see that," she says. "But what is so exciting about a period?"

"Damned if I know!" answers Little Johnny, "but this morning my sis told us she missed one. Right afterwards, my father had a heart attack…my mother fainted…and the man next door shot himself!"

PREPARE YOURSELF…

Little Johnny walks into Old Man Taylor's store one Friday evening to buy some condoms. The pharmacist in the back of the store asks him which pack he wants and explains that the condoms come in packs of three, six and twelve.

"Well," Little Johnny explains, "I've been seeing this girl for a while now. We're having dinner with her parents tonight and then we're goin' to the dollar movie. I'm sure after all that I'm gonna get lucky…you better give me the twelve pack!"

Later that evening, Little Johnny sits down to dinner with his girlfriend Lanie and her parents. Little Johnny insists that he give the blessing and they all agree. As he clears his throat to begin, Lanie leans over and whispers, "You never told me you were such a religious person."

Little Johnny replies, "You never told me your father was a pharmacist!"

SURE IS DARK IN HERE...

Little Johnny's mother is having an affair. Whenever her lover comes over, she puts Little Johnny in the bedroom closet. One day, as she hears her husband coming up the stairs, she shoves her lover in the closet with Little Johnny.

"Gee, it sure is dark in here?" whispers Little Johnny.

"Yes it is," the man replies.

"You wanna buy a football for a hundred dollars?" Little Johnny asks.

"One hundred dollars?" the man repeats. Acknowledging his position, the man quickly forks over the money.

A few days later, Little Johnny's father says, "Son, go get your football."

"I can't...I sold it," replies Little Johnny.

"How much did you get for it?" asks his father.

"A hundred dollars," replies Little Johnny.

"One hundred dollars? Who on earth gave you that kind of money?" Little Johnny is silent. "Well, if you're not going to tell me, then you can ask for forgiveness at confession!"

Once at the church, Little Johnny enters the confessional booth, draws the curtain and sits down. "Gee, it sure is dark in here?" he whispers.

"Please don't start that crap again!" pleads the priest.

IN LOVING MEMORY...

One Sunday morning, Father Harrison notices Little Johnny staring up at the large plaque just inside the church foyer, "You know, Little Johnny, that plaque is a memorial to all of the young men and women who died in the service."

Soberly they stood together, staring at the large plaque. After a short while, Johnny decides to ask, "Which service did they die in...the 9:00AM or the 10:30AM?"

ENGLISH COMPOSITION...

During English class, Miss Jones states, "In the English language, a double negative forms a positive. On the other hand, in Russian, a double negative is still a negative. With that said, there is no language where a double positive can form a negative."

Little Johnny clears his throat and says, "Yeah, right."

PRIVATE PARTS...

One Saturday, Little Johnny and his parents decide to go to the circus. Once they've found their seats, his father heads for the concession stand. Before long, a large elephant is brought into the ring. Suddenly, Little Johnny begins jumping up and down and points, "Mommy, Mommy, what's that?"

"That's the elephant's trunk," she answers.

Still pointing, Little Johnny cries out, "No, on the other end!"

"That's its tail.

"No, under that!"

Embarrassed, his mother replies, "It's nothing!" and quickly tries to change the subject.

As soon as Little Johnny's father returns with everyone's drinks and popcorn, his mother excuses herself to the restroom.

Noticing the elephants again, Little Johnny tugs on his father's sleeve, "Daddy, Daddy, what's that?"

"The trunk."

"No, on the other end."

"The tail."

"No, under that!"

"That's the elephant's penis, son."

Little Johnny thinks for a moment and says, "But Mommy just told me it was nothin'."

"Well son…your mother's pretty spoiled."

FROZEN TURKEYS…

Little Johnny decided it would be a good idea to pick up some quick cash over the summer by working as a stock boy at the local grocery store. One afternoon, a lady was picking through the frozen turkeys for an unusually long time before asking, "Do these turkeys get any bigger?"

Little Johnny thinks for a minute and says, "No ma'am they're dead."

HOW NOW BROWN COW…

Uncle J.R. owns a brown cow and a white cow. One day he decides that he wants to breed them, so he borrows his neighbor's bull and turns it loose in the pasture. He asks Little Johnny to watch for a while and to let him know when the bull is finished.

A few hours later, Little Johnny comes into the living room where his uncle is talking with some friends.

"Hey, Uncle J.R.," says Little Johnny.

"Yes," replies his uncle.

"The bull just screwed the brown cow!"

Needless to say, there is a sudden lull in the conversation. Uncle J.R. is somewhat embarrassed and excuses himself. He leads Little Johnny back outside and explains, "Boy, you mustn't use language like that in front of company. You should say 'The bull surprised the brown cow.' Now get back out there and this time let me know when the bull surprises the white cow."

Uncle J.R. hesitantly goes back inside. Not much time has passed when Little Johnny returns to the living room, "Hey, Uncle J.R."

"Did the bull surprise the white cow?" asks his uncle.

"He sure did, Uncle J.R.! He screwed the brown cow again!"

LUNCH DATE...

Miss Jones was a little unsure how well her students would respond to her Geography lesson, but she was determined to get through to them. Following a detailed lecture on longitude and latitude, Miss Jones posed the following question, "Where would I be if I asked you to meet me for lunch at 23 degrees latitude and 45 degrees longitude?"

After an awkward and prolonged silence, Little Johnny decides to speak up, "I guess you'd be eating alone."

BEYOND BIRDS AND BEES...

One morning when his mother is in the kitchen cooking breakfast, Little Johnny asks, "Mommy, where do babies come from?"

"Well dear," she explains, "A Mommy and Daddy fall in love and get married. Eventually, they go to their bedroom...kiss and hug and have sex."

Little Johnny looks very puzzled at this point.

His mother continues, "That means that a Daddy puts his penis in a Mommy's vagina. That's how you get a baby."

"Oh, I see," says Little Johnny. "Well how about the other night when I came into your bedroom...you had Daddy's peter in your mouth. What do you get when you do that?"

"Jewelry dear," answers his mother.

ENJOY IT WHILE YOU CAN...

Little Johnny and his father are in Old Man Taylor's store one afternoon when they happen upon the condom aisle. Rather curious, Little Johnny asks his father, "Why are there so many different boxes of condoms?"

His father replies, "Well...you see that three pack? That's for when you're in high school...two for Friday night and one for Saturday night."

"What about the six pack?" asks Little Johnny.

His father continues, "Well...that's for when you're in college... two for Friday night, two for Saturday night, and two for Sunday night."

"What's the twelve pack for?" asks Little Johnny.

"Well son…that's for when you're married. You have one for January, one for February, one for March.…"

FAIR WARNING…

Noticing that Little Johnny is making ugly faces at some of the other children while on the playground, Miss Jones takes him by the arm and says, "Little Johnny, when I was a child, I was told that if I made ugly faces, my face would freeze, and stay like that permanently."

Little Johnny looks up and replies, "Well…you can't say you weren't warned."

BARE NECESSITIES…

Little Johnny comes home from school with a note from his teacher, "Little Johnny seems to be having some difficulty understanding the differences between boys and girls. Please sit down and have a talk with Little Johnny about this."

After reading this, Little Johnny's mother leads him upstairs to her bedroom and closes the door.

"First, Little Johnny, I want you to take off my blouse.…"

So he unbuttons her blouse and takes it off.

"OK, now take off my skirt.…"

And he takes off her skirt.

"Now take off my bra...."

Which he does.

"And now, Little Johnny, please take off my panties."

When Little Johnny finishes removing this, she says, "Little Johnny, please don't wear any of my clothes to school anymore!"

YOUTHFUL EXUBERANCE...

Miss Jones is concerned with one of her students. Taking him aside after class one day, she asks, "Little Johnny, why has your school work been so poor lately?"

"I'm in love," the boy replies.

Holding back the urge to smile, she asks, "With whom?"

"With you," he says.

"But Little Johnny," she explains, "don't you see how silly that is? It's true that I would like a husband of my own someday, but I don't want a child."

"Oh, don't worry," the boy says reassuringly, "I'll use a rubber."

OCCUPATIONAL HAZZARD...

Miss Jones asks her students to name and spell what one of their parents does for a living.

First up is Nikki. "My Mommy is a nurse. Nurse is spelled n-u-r-s-e."

Scotty is next. "My Dad is an electrician. You spell electrician e-l-a-k…uhhh…

e-l-e-x…uhhh…"

Miss Jones quickly comforts Scotty, "Think about it for a while and we will come back to you. Little Johnny, you are next."

Little Johnny proceeds, "My Daddy is a bookie. That's b-o-o-k-i-e and I'll lay ten-to-one odds that Scotty don't ever spell electrician!"

DATE OF BIRTH…

While registering for the fall soccer league, one of the volunteers asks Little Johnny, "What is your date of birth?"

"May fourteenth," Little Johnny answers.

"What year?"

"Every year."

CLOSING THE SALE…

Little Johnny walks into Old Man Taylor's store one Saturday and asks Mr. Taylor for a job. Impressed by the boy's candor, Old Man Taylor asks Little Johnny to familiarize himself with the manner in which he helps the next customer. If Little Johnny can obtain similar results with the following customer then he would in turn give him a job.

Shortly after, Old Man Taylor approaches a gentleman entering his store, "Good afternoon sir. What can I do for you?"

"I need some grass seed," the gentleman replies.

As Old Man Taylor fetches the grass seed he asks, "How about a lawn mower to go with this grass seed?"

"Now, what would I need a lawn mower for?" he replies.

"Well, when this seed starts to kick in, your grass will be so tall and dense you'll need a lawn mower to trim it back."

Nodding his head in agreement, the gentleman replies, "You're probably right...a lawn mower will come in handy...I'll take it."

While ringing up the sale, Old Man Taylor winks at Little Johnny and says, "That's how it's done kid...can you do that?"

Little Johnny is quite confident as he greets the next customer, "Good afternoon, sir. What can I do for you?"

"I need some tampons," the gentleman replies.

As Little Johnny fetches the tampons he asks, "Would you like a lawn mower to go with that?"

"What the hell do I need a lawn mower for?"

"Well you might as well cut the grass...'cause your weekend's shot...that's for sure!"

THE NAKED TRUTH...

Little Johnny and Lanie are playing in the sandbox when they start having an argument about boys and girls. Clearly frustrated, Little Johnny finally stands up, drops his trousers and boasts, "Boys are better than girls 'cause you ain't got one of these!"

Lanie is shocked. She knows she doesn't have one of those between her legs, so she bursts out crying and rushes inside to her mother. After a short while, Lanie returns to the sandbox and says with a big grin on her face, "My Mommy says girls are definitely better than boys."

"No they're not," says Little Johnny...dropping his trousers again, "You haven't got one of these!"

Lanie looks him up and down...raises her skirt...pulls down her panties...and says, "My Mommy says that as long as I've got one of these...I can have as many of those as I want!"

CONFESSION...

One morning in Sunday school, Sister Mathews asks Little Johnny, "Do you know where young boys and girls go when they do bad things?"

"Sure," Little Johnny replies. "They go out in back of the church yard."

FULL HOUSE...

Little Johnny wakes up in the middle of the night having to go to the bathroom. On his way, he passes his parents room. As he looks in, it appears that their covers are bouncing up and down. Curious, he asks, "Hey Daddy, what are you doing?"

His father answers, "Playing cards."

"Who's your partner?" Little Johnny asks.

"Your Mom is," answers his father.

As he proceeds down the hall, Little Johnny passes his sister's room. Again, it appears that her covers are bouncing up and down. "Hey sis, what are you doing?"

His sister answers, "Playing cards."

"Who's your partner?" Little Johnny asks.

"Don't tell Mom and Dad, but it's my boyfriend," answers his sister.

Later that same evening, Little Johnny's father heads downstairs to the kitchen. As he passes Little Johnny's room, he can't help but notice that his covers appear to be bouncing up and down. He calls to his son, "What are you doing?"

Little Johnny answers, "Playing cards."

"Really? Who's your partner?" his father asks.

"You don't need a partner if you have a good hand!" answers Little Johnny.

CHORE WARS...

Little Johnny's parents figure sending their son to Uncle J.R. and Aunt J.J.'s farm for the weekend will give them just the break they need.

The very first morning, Uncle J.R. says, "Little Johnny, I'd like you to go feed the animals." Little Johnny, somewhat irritated, gets out of bed and walks past his aunt who is making breakfast in the kitchen. Little Johnny scornfully gathers the food for the farm animals.

First, Little Johnny enters the henhouse...kicks the chickens and throws their feed to the ground. Next, Little Johnny sneaks up to the pig, kicks it, and drops its slop in the trough. Lastly, Little Johnny approaches the cow...kicks it, and scatters its food from one end of the pasture to the other. Meanwhile, his aunt can see all of what Little Johnny is doing from the kitchen.

As Little Johnny enters the house, his aunt says, "I saw what you did. For kicking the chickens, you will have no eggs for breakfast;

for kicking the pig, you will have no bacon; and for kicking the cow, you will have no milk."

Meanwhile, Little Johnny's uncle walks down the stairs, trips over the cat and nearly falls. He swiftly kicks the cat.

Little Johnny looks at his aunt and says, "Should I tell him what he's not gettin', or do you wanna tell him?"

MATH FEARING...

Little Johnny is having just a terrible time with his mathematics. Both his parents work with him night after night...but there is no improvement. Although neither parent is terribly religious, they decide to transfer Little Johnny to St. Francis...a local Catholic School with an outstanding academic reputation.

Immediately Little Johnny's math marks begin to soar. Naturally, this dramatic improvement has his parents curious as to what approach St. Francis uses that Little Johnny's previous school doesn't. "Are the teachers at St. Francis more demanding?" they ask.

"No, the teachers are about the same," Little Johnny replies.

"Are the text books better?" they ask.

"No, we're actually using the same text book," Little Johnny replies.

"So why are you suddenly making A's in math?" his parents ask.

"I know if I don't there would be serious consequences…ones I don't ever wanna deal with."

"What makes you think that?"

"Well, the very first thing I saw when I went into math class was a statue of some guy nailed to a plus sign!"

NOT FAR FROM THE TREE…

One day, for snack time, Miss Jones brings her class some cookies. "Here Little Johnny," she gestures, "have a cookie."

"I don't want a damn cookie," declares Little Johnny.

Needless to say, Miss Jones is quite offended by this remark. That afternoon, she phones Little Johnny's mother and asks her to come in the next morning for a meeting. Upon arrival, Miss Jones has his mother stand outside the classroom door…just far enough that the class can be heard but not seen. Miss Jones then proceeds to approach Little Johnny with a new batch of cookies.

"Here Little Johnny," she gestures, "have a cookie."

"I don't want a damn cookie," declares Little Johnny.

Immediately Miss Jones fetches Little Johnny's mother and sternly asks, "There, did you hear what he just said to me?"

His mother shrugs her shoulders…"So don't give him a damn cookie."

URINATE...

Little Johnny is sitting in class one day. All of a sudden, he needs to go to the bathroom. He yells out, "Miss Jones, I need to take a piss!"

The teacher replies, "Now, Little Johnny, that is not the proper word to use in this situation. The word you want to use is urinate. Please use the word urinate in a sentence correctly, and I will allow you to go."

Little Johnny thinks for a bit, and then says, "You're an eight, but if you had bigger tits, you'd be a ten!"

MISTAKEN IDENTITY...

Little Johnny is concerned, "Mommy, tomorrow I have an oral exam. One of the questions Miss Jones will be asking is, 'who made you.' What should I tell her?"

His mother replies, "Tell her that God made you."

The next day, when asked the question, Little Johnny has a hard time remembering what his Mom told him the night before and answers, "Miss Jones, I was sure it was my Daddy who made me until yesterday. That's when my Mommy told me it was someone else. Right now though, I can't remember his name."

PEEP SHOW...

Little Johnny and his two buddies, Billy and Scotty, are walking home from school one warm spring afternoon. All of a sudden they notice a small hole in one of the fences bordering the walkway. Each of them takes turns looking through the hole and to their amazement...there is a beautiful woman sunbathing in the nude. Suddenly, Little Johnny begins to scream, takes off running and leaves his buddies.

The next day, the three boys follow the same identical path and once more stare at the beautiful woman through the fence hole. After just a few minutes, Little Johnny again begins screaming and quickly runs off.

On the third day, Billy and Scotty are determined to find out why Little Johnny keeps pitching a fit following this new custom of theirs. As the boys are peeping through the fence-hole...like clockwork...Little Johnny begins to scream and takes off running. This time, however, Billy and Scotty chase him down, grab him and demand to know why he keeps acting this way.

Little Johnny nervously replies, "My mother told me that if I ever looked at a naked woman, I would turn to stone, and I started to feel a part of me getting awfully hard...."

NEW MEMBER OF THE CLASS...

Miss Jones enters her classroom one morning and finds a drawing of a penis on the blackboard. She suspiciously eyeballs the class and quickly rubs it off.

The next morning, there is another drawing of even a bigger penis on the blackboard. This time Miss Jones frowns a bit, then rubs it off.

The following morning, she once again finds a drawing of a penis. This drawing is huge, covering more than half the blackboard.

This was about all Miss Jones could take, "Who keeps drawing this penis on the blackboard every day? And why does it keep getting bigger?"

Little Johnny quickly responds, "The more you rub it, the bigger it gets!"

SEXUALLY INACTIVE...

It's the first year Little Johnny's been old enough to participate at his school's blood drive. While going over a few questions, the nurse asks, "Are you sexually active?"

Little Johnny quickly replies, "No...I just lie there."

TERMINAL ILLNESS...

Little Johnny and his mother arrive at the airport earlier than expected, so they have a little time before his father's plane touches down. While they wait, Little Johnny's mother decides it's a good time to give him some encouragement, "I know how much you enjoy sleeping in the same bed as me when you're father is out of town. So I must say, I'm very proud of you for sleeping on your own during your father's latest trip…and I can't wait for him to find out the good news."

Once the plane arrives, everyone gathers as passengers begin to slowly enter the terminal. As his father approaches through the crowd, Little Johnny shouts, "Dad! I've got great news…nobody slept with Mommy while you were away this time!"

BEAUTIFUL…

One morning Miss Jones says, "Children, I am going to ask each of you to come to the front of the class and use the word beautiful in a complete sentence. Nikki, would you please come up here and use beautiful in a sentence?"

Nikki walks to the front of the room, thinks for a moment and says, "My Mom is the most beautiful woman in the world."
Miss Jones responds, "Very good Nikki, you may sit…Scotty, your turn."

Scotty walks to the front of the room, thinks for a moment and says, "The sunrise this morning was the most beautiful sunrise I have ever seen."

"Very good Scotty," says Miss Jones, "You may sit…Little Johnny, you're next."

Little Johnny casually walks to the front of the classroom and without hesitation says, "Last night my sis told my father that she was pregnant and he said 'Beautiful, just beautiful.'"

TRICK QUESTION...

In a very passive tone, Little Johnny hesitantly asks Miss Jones, "Would you punish me for something I didn't do?"

"Of course not," Miss Jones replies.

"Great, because I didn't do my homework!"

YOU GOTTA BELIEVE...

One evening, after being asked by his father if he knows about the birds and the bees, Little Johnny bursts into tears. Confused, his father asks, "What's wrong son?"

Showing obvious disappointment, Little Johnny replies, "I found out that there was no Santa Claus at age six...no Easter Bunny at age seven...and no Tooth Fairy at age eight. So if you're fixin' to tell me that grownups don't really have sex, then I've got nothin' left to believe in!"

HARASSMENT...

Miss Jones asks Little Johnny to use the word harassment in a sentence.

Little Johnny replies, "Her mouth said no, but her ass meant yes!"

MONKEY SEE, MONKEY DO...

A few months after his parents are divorced, Little Johnny passes by his mother's bedroom and sees her rubbing her body and moaning, "Ohh, I need a man, I need a man!" Over the next couple of months, he sees her doing this several times. One day, he comes home from school and hears her once again. This time when he peeks into her bedroom, he sees a man on top of her. Immediately, Little Johnny runs into his room, takes off his clothes, throws himself on his bed and starts rubbing his body and moaning, "Ohh, I need a bike! I need a bike!"

CHIP OFF THE OLD BLOCK...

Little Johnny returns home from school one afternoon and explains to his father that he got an 'F' on his math test.

"Why?" asks his father.

"Well, Miss Jones asked me how much 2x3 equaled...and I said 6."

"But that's right!" exclaims his father.

"Well, then she asked me how much 3x2 equaled."

"What the hell is the difference?"

"That's exactly what I said!"

ROUGHING IT...

On the first day of summer camp, the Head Counselor addresses the youngsters, pointing out some of the rules:

"The female bunks are off limits to all males and the male bunks are off limits to all females. Anybody caught breaking this rule will be fined $20 the first time. Anyone caught breaking this rule a second time will be fined $60. A third time will cost you $100. Do any of you have any questions?"

Little Johnny bravely clears his throat and asks, "How much for a season pass?"

TONGUE-TIED...

Little Johnny walks into his parents bedroom one evening only to catch his father sitting on the side of the bed sliding a condom onto his peter. In an attempt to downplay this awkward moment, his father bends over as if to look under the bed.

Little Johnny asks curiously, "Whatcha doin', Dad?"

His father quickly replies, "I thought I saw a rat go underneath the bed."

To which Little Johnny replies, "Whatcha gonna do, screw him?"

A GOOD SPANKING…

Little Johnny is becoming a real nuisance as his father tries to concentrate on his Saturday afternoon poker game with friends and relatives. His father tries every way possible to get Little Johnny to occupy himself…television, ice cream, homework, video games…but the youngster insists on running back and forth behind the players…blurting out the cards they hold.

The other players become so annoyed that they threaten to quit the game and all go home. At this point, the boy's Uncle J.R. stands up, takes Little Johnny by the hand, and leads him out of the room. His uncle soon returns to the poker table without Little Johnny.

For the rest of the afternoon, Little Johnny is nowhere to be seen and the card players are able to continue without any further interruptions.

After the poker game ends, the father asks Uncle J.R., "What in the world did you say to Little Johnny? I haven't heard a peep from him all day!"

"Not much," the boy's uncle replies, "I just showed him how to masturbate."

RELIGION 101…

Sister Mathews is concerned that her students might be a little confused about the true meaning of Christmas. With all the commercialism that now surrounds the holidays, Sister Mathews wants to make sure they understand Christmas from a religious standpoint. With this in mind, she asks the class, "Where is Jesus today?"

Mike raises his hand and says, "He's in Heaven."

Lanie is next. She answers, "He's in my heart."

Little Johnny, speaking out of turn, says, "I know! I know! He's in our bathroom!"

The whole class gets very quiet. Sister Mathews is thoroughly confused…after gathering her wits, she asks, "Little Johnny what makes you think that Jesus is in your bathroom?"

"Well…every morning, my father gets up, bangs on the bathroom door and yells 'Jesus Christ, are you still in there?'"

DO AS THEY SAY, NOT AS THEY DO…

While watching TV one evening with his friend Jarrod, Little Johnny begins to notice some odd behavior out of his parents…a wink here…and a nod there. Eventually, his Mom says, "Your Dad and I are going upstairs for a few minutes, but we'll be right back…so stay right here."

A few minutes later, Little Johnny motions for Jarrod to follow him upstairs. As they tiptoe toward his parent's bedroom, Little Johnny whispers, "Before I show you what they're doing…keep in mind…this is the same woman that used to scold me for sucking my thumb!"

CAREER DAY...

Following church on Sunday morning, Little Johnny announces to his mother, "Mommy, I've decided I'm going to be a minister when I grow up."

"That's perfectly fine with us," she says, "But what made you decide to become a minister?"

"Well," Little Johnny replies, "I'm forced go to church every Sunday anyway...so I figured it might be more fun to stand up and yell...than sit still and listen."

A PERFECT GENTLEMAN...

One evening at supper, Little Johnny mentions to his mother, "Mommy, when I was on the bus this morning, Daddy asked me to give up my seat to a lady standing nearby."

His Mom is overjoyed and says, "Son, you did the right thing...I'm very proud of you!"

Hesitantly, Little Johnny responds, "But Mommy, I was sitting on Daddy's lap at the time."

A HISTORY LEASON...

During Geography class, Miss Jones asks Missy to find America on the classroom map.

Missy eyeballs the map for a few of minutes and finally says, "Here it is!"

"That's correct Missy," says Miss Jones. "Now, who can tell me who discovered America?"

Little Johnny immediately jumps to his feet and proclaims, "Well duh… Missy did!"

NEW MATH…

During Math Class, Miss Jones asks Little Johnny, "If you received $10 from ten people, what would you get?"

Little Johnny quickly answers, "A new bike!"

REVERSE PSYCHOLOGY…

One day, Miss Jones thought she would pass along some of the knowledge that she has gained during her many Psychology courses. She begins the class by announcing, "Everyone who thinks they're stupid, please stand up."

After a few minutes, Little Johnny slowly stands up.

"Do you think you're stupid, Little Johnny?" she asks.

"No ma'am," he says, "but I hate to see you standing there all by yourself."

PUPPY LOVE…

Little Johnny and his father are strolling through the park one Saturday when they see two dogs mating. Little Johnny is not quite sure what is happening and asks, "Daddy, what are those two dogs doing?"

To which his father replies, "They're making a puppy."

Later that same night, Little Johnny wakes up having to go to the bathroom. As he passes his parent's bedroom, he sees his parents locked in a sexual embrace. "Daddy," he says, "what are you and Mommy doing?"

To which his father replies, "We're making you a little sister."

Little Johnny thinks for a moment and responds, "Well Daddy, could you roll her over? I'd rather have a puppy!"

ALL ABOARD…

A few days after Christmas, Little Johnny's mother is working in the kitchen while her son plays with his new electric train set in the living room. Suddenly, she hears the train stop and Little Johnny announce:

"All you sons-of-bitches who are gettin' off, get your asses in gear. And, all you sons-of-bitches who are gettin' on, you'd better do the same 'cause we're leaving!"

His mother immediately rushes into the living room and scolds Little Johnny, "We don't use that kind of language in this house! Now, I want you to go up to your room for two hours. Only then may you come downstairs and play with your train…and only if you use appropriate language."

Two hours later, Little Johnny returns and resumes playing with his train. Soon the train stops and his mother hears Little Johnny announce:

"All passengers disembarking the train, please remember to take all of your belongings with you. We thank you for riding with us today and hope that you will ride with us again soon. For those of you just boarding, we ask that you stow all of your carry-on luggage under your seat or in the overhead bins. We sincerely hope that you will have a pleasant and relaxing journey with us today. For those inconvenienced by the two hour delay…please see the bitch in the kitchen!"

1 + 1 = 1…

Working her way around the room, Miss Jones finally gets around to asking Little Johnny his math question for the day, "If you had one dollar and you asked your father for another, how many dollars would you have?"

With no hesitation, Little Johnny answers, "One dollar!"

"You don't know your arithmetic," replies Miss Jones.

"No," says Little Johnny, "You don't know my father!"

SIGN LANGUAGE…

Somewhat afraid of the answer, Miss Jones asks Little Johnny, "And just why are you late young man?"

"Because of the sign," answers Little Johnny.

"And what sign is that?"

"The one that says 'school ahead, go slow'…so that's what I did!"

ROUGH DRAFT…

Little Johnny's parents decide it would be a good idea for him to spend a day with the family pastor. As Little Johnny watches Father Harrison jot down ideas for the following week's sermon, he asks, "How do you decide what to write down Father Harrison?"

"Well son," he answers, "God tells me what to write down."

"Then why do you keep crossing things out?"

ORAL EXAM…

Since Little Johnny spent much of the morning in the principal's office, he missed the pop test Miss Jones had planed for the class. Miss Jones made up for this by giving Little Johnny his own test during lunch period.

Miss Jones begins, "Now Little Johnny, all of your responses must be oral for this makeup test, OK? The first question is, 'What is the capital of South Carolina?'"

Without missing a beat, Little Johnny answers, "Oral."

ADVENTURES IN BABYSITTING...

One morning in Sunday school, Father Harrison asks the class if any of them know why Joseph and Mary took Baby Jesus with them on their trip to Jerusalem.

Although a little unsure of himself, Little Johnny answers, "They couldn't get a baby sitter?"

ERASER...

Miss Jones writes 10.9 on the blackboard and then erases the decimal point to show the result of multiplying this number by ten. She then asks, "Little Johnny, where is the decimal point now?"

Little Johnny answers, "It's on the eraser!"

SCHOOL PLAY...

Knowing parts for the school play were announced recently, Little Johnny's Dad asks, "Son, were you able to get a part in this year's play?"

Little Johnny enthusiastically answers, "I sure did...I play a man who's been married for twenty years...and they said if keep up the good work, I may can even work my way up to a speaking part!"

THE NAME GAME...

Little Johnny is excited to hear the news that he will soon have a younger sister or brother, and while his parents don't share all the details with him, he does occasionally overhear some things he shouldn't. Well, one day, Little Johnny and his mother are at the checkout counter, when one of their neighbors asks Little Johnny if he is looking forward to having a new sibling soon.

"I sure am!" exclaims Little Johnny. "And I know what we're naming the baby too...if it's a girl, we're going to call her Millie... and if it's a boy we're going to call him Quits!"

DO YOU BELIEVE?

Miss Jones drops a bombshell on her students one afternoon, "I'm proud to say I'm an atheist. Are there any other atheists in the room?"

Afraid of what Miss Jones will do to them if they respond any differently, every student raises their hand...every student except for Little Johnny.

In turn, Miss Jones looks directly at Little Johnny and sternly asks, "Well, what are you, if you're not an atheist?"

"Well, since my mother and father are Christians, I guess that would make me a Christian."

"What if your mother and father were morons, what would that make you?"

"I guess that would make me an atheist."

LET'S PLAY DOCTOR?

At recess one day, Lanie asks Little Johnny, "Hey, do you wanna get undressed and play Doctor?"

"That's too old fashioned," replies Little Johnny. "Spit out your gum and let's play President!"

FLASH CARDS...

Knowing she probably wouldn't get a straight answer, Miss Jones asks Little Johnny, "Did you study your flash cards last night like you were supposed to?"

"I sure did," Little Johnny replies. "My father helped me with them."

"OK. So what comes after three?"

"Four!"

"Correct. What comes after six?"

"Seven!"

"Very good. Your father did a good job. What comes after ten?"

"A Jack!"

MOTHER'S DAY...

Miss Jones asks her class what each of them is getting for their moms for Mother's Day. When she gets to Little Johnny, he explains that he really wants to get his mom something special, but he's just having a hard time coming up with what that something is.

"Well do you know what her favorite flower is?" asks Miss Jones.

"Well, I'm pretty sure it's Pillsbury," replies Little Johnny.

HARMONICA...

Because Little Johnny hadn't seen his Uncle J.R. since before Christmas, he decides it would be nice to thank him for his present, "Thanks for the harmonica you gave me Uncle J.R.! It has to be one of the best Christmas presents I've ever gotten!"

"I'm happy to hear it young fella," says his uncle. "Have you learned how to play that thing yet?"

"Oh no, I don't play it," replies Little Johnny, "In fact, Mommy gives me an allowance not to play it."

O...

While going through the alphabet letter-by-letter, Miss Jones finally gets around to Little Johnny and asks, "What comes after 'O'?"

"Yea!" answers Little Johnny.

STRAIGHT…

Miss Jones asks Little Johnny to spell the word straight…and he does so without a hitch.

"Now," says Miss Jones, "Do you know what that word means?"

"All alcohol and no mixer?" Little Johnny responds.

COIN TOSS…

By the time Little Johnny arrives at Billy's birthday party, all of the door prizes had already been given away. "Why are you so late?" Billy asks.

"Well, I decided to toss a coin to decide between going to church and coming here," replies Little Johnny.

"How long could that have taken you?"

"Well, I had to toss it eleven times."

JUVENILE JEOPARDY…

One day, Miss Jones walks into her classroom and announces, "Beginning this Friday, I will ask the class a question. Whoever answers it correctly does not have to come to school the following Monday."

On the first Friday, the teacher asks, "How many grains of sand are on the beach?" Needless to say, no one could answer. The following Friday, the teacher asks the class, "How many stars are in the sky?" And again no one could answer. Frustrated, Little Johnny decides that the next Friday, he would somehow answer the question and get a three-day weekend. So Thursday night, Little Johnny takes two ping-pong balls and paints them black. The next day, he brings them to school in a paper bag. At the end of the day…just when the teacher says, "Here's this week's question," Little Johnny empties the bag onto the floor, sending the ping-pong balls rolling to the front of the classroom. The entire class starts laughing.

The teacher asks, "OK, who's the comedian with the black balls?"

Immediately, Little Johnny stands up and says, "Bill Cosby! See ya on Tuesday!"

WEDDING BELL BLUES…

Attending a wedding for the first time, Little Johnny whispers to his mother, "Mommy, why's the bride dressed in white?"

"Because white is the color of happiness and today is the happiest day of her life."

Little Johnny thinks about his mother's answer for a moment, then adds, "So why's the groom wearing black?"

RISKY BUSINESS…

A traveling salesman rings the doorbell and Little Johnny leisurely opens the door…wearing only a pair of boxer-shorts, holding a beer and smoking a fat cigar. The salesman hesitantly asks, "Is your mother home?"

Little Johnny taps his ash on the carpet and says, "What do you think?"

COLUMBUS DAY...

After concluding a condensed story about how Columbus discovered America, Miss Jones says, "And all this happened more than five hundred years ago."

"Gosh!" exclaims Little Johnny, "What a great memory you have!"

STORKS...

Immediately after getting off the school bus, Little Johnny storms through the front door of his house and hollers out angrily, "Everyone within earshot listen up, because I'm only going to say this once! Be advised that I...Little Johnny...made a complete and utter fool of myself in sex education class today. How, you might ask? Well, it was due to the extreme confidence I showed while repeating a certain story about storks as told to me by persons residing in this very house!"

ABSENCE...

Little Johnny's mother disappointingly stares at a big red 'F' on Little Johnny's latest math test. "Why such a low grade son?"

"Because of an absence," Little Johnny answers.

"You mean you were absent on the day of the test?"

"No…but the kid who sits next to me was."

WHAT'S HE LIKE?

After chasing one of his classmates through the crowded mall, Little Johnny suddenly realizes his Uncle J.R. is no longer within sight. He therefore approaches one of the mall security guards and sadly says, "I can't seem to find my uncle. And he's my only ride home."

"What's he like?" asks the guard.

"Beer and women."

SOUP OF THE DAY…

Little Johnny is waiting tables over summer break when Old Man Taylor sits down in the only booth still available in his section.

"Would you care for our soup of the day Mr. Taylor?" asks Little Johnny.

"No, I would rather have something I can sink my teeth in", Old Man Taylor explains.

"Oh, then you want a glass of water?"

SLEEPYHEAD...

Shortly after Miss Jones hands out this week's science test, she notices Little Johnny with his head on his desk. Thinking she's caught him sleeping, Miss Jones clears her throat and says, "Little Johnny, what do you think you're doing?"

Startled out of his slumber, Little Johnny gets his wits about him, slowly raises his head and says, "In Jesus' name, Amen."

HAM SANDWICH...

Instead of sitting by his parents on the plane ride to Disney World, Little Johnny instead sits by what turns out to be a rabbi. After settling into their seats, Little Johnny asks, "Is it still a requirement of your faith that you not eat pork?"

"Yes that is still part of our faith," replies the rabbi.

"Have you ever slipped up and eaten pork?"

"Yes, there was a time recently when I tasted a ham sandwich."

"Is it still a requirement of your faith that you remain celibate?"

"Yes, that also is still part of our faith."

"Have you slipped up in that area?"

"I must be honest. Yes, on one occasion I was weak and broke with my faith in this area."

"Beats a ham sandwich, doesn't it?"

BUNK BEDS...

Little Johnny was staying with his Uncle J.R. and Aunt J.J. over spring break when he asks his uncle, "What is it called when two people are sleeping, one on top of the other?"

Taken somewhat aback, Uncle J.R. decides to give an honest answer, "Well, it's called sexual intercourse."

Not sure he completely understands, Little Johnny decides to just head to the kitchen for a snack. A few minutes later, Little Johnny returns and says loudly, "Aunt J.J. says it's not called sexual intercourse... its called bunk beds! And she wants you in the kitchen right now!"

CAN YOU HEAR ME NOW?

Little Johnny steps onto the back porch, opens the door and screams into the house, "Mommy! Hey Mommy!"

Obviously irritated, his Mom yells back, "Little Johnny, stop yelling in this house! If you want to talk to me, walk over to the living room where I'm at!"

As he walks onto the living room carpet, Little Johnny looks down at his feet and says, "I stepped in dog poop...do you know where the hose is?"

911…

Little Johnny is in the middle of playing his new video game when he smells smoke. In fact, the smell is overwhelming and as he looks outside he sees his neighbor's house on fire. Remembering what he was taught, he rushes to the phone, calls 911 and says, "Hurry! Our neighbor's house is on fire!"

Immediately, the dispatcher asks, "Stay calm son…and tell us how to get there?"

"Well can't you just use a fire truck?"

QUICKIE…

One morning, Little Johnny and his mother are having breakfast at the local diner. An attractive waitress approaches their table and asks Little Johnny, "What would like young man?"

"How about a quickie?" replies Little Johnny.

Obviously embarrassed, Little Johnny's mother leans over to her son and whispers, "Its pronounced quiche."

PLAY DATE…

Miss Jones has been very disappointed in her class' behavior of late, so following a brief lecture on the subject, she asks, "If you're on a play date, how would you tell the other person that you have to go to the bathroom?"

Little Johnny seizes the moment and answers, "May I please be excused for a moment? I must shake hands with a dear friend of mine...one whom I hope you'll meet later tonight."

VARICOSE...

Having already misspelled the word, Miss Jones asks Little Johnny if he even knows what the word varicose means.

Little Johnny confidently answers, "Nearby."

POOL SIDE...

Little Johnny is at the neighborhood pool one Saturday when a lifeguard reluctantly approaches him and begins to fuss, "Little Johnny, how many times do I have to tell you not to pee in the pool?"

"But everybody does it," claims Little Johnny.

"Not standing from the diving board they don't!" utters the lifeguard.

INSERT FOOT HERE...

Little Johnny's parents drop him off at the front of the church and ask him to go ahead and find them all a seat while they park the car.

As Little Johnny approaches the sanctuary, the usher asks, "Where would you like to sit?"

"Anywhere but the front row, cause I gotta tell you, Father Harrison's sermons are beyond boring!"

"Do you know who I am?"

"No."

"I'm Father Harrison's nephew."

"Do you know who I am?"

"No."

"Good."

SHOW AND TELL...

Miss Jones thought it would be educational to have her class bring in an item that best represents their religion.

Stephanie begins, "I'm Jewish and this is a Star of David."

Sherry is next and says, "I'm a Catholic and this is a Rosary."

Not to be outdone, Little Johnny says, "I'm a Baptist, and I brought this here casserole!"

MAN'S BEST FRIEND…

Old Man Taylor is walking down the sidewalk and notices up ahead that Little Johnny is wearing a shiny red fireman's hat and sitting in a little red wagon. It appears that the wagon is being pulled rather gingerly by Little Johnny's dog Freckles. As the old man gets closer to the lad, he notices that Little Johnny has tied a rope around the dog's testicles.

As he smiles, the old man says, "That's really a nice fire engine you have there son. But I'll bet Freckles would pull you faster if you tied that rope around his neck instead."

"Yeah," Little Johnny replies, "but then I wouldn't have a siren!"

PSSST…

Little Johnny returns from recess and proceeds to tell Miss Jones that he found a dead cat by the swing set. "How do you know the cat was dead?" she asks.

"Because I pissed in its ear and it didn't move," answers Little Johnny.

"You did what?"

"You know…I leaned over close to the cat's ear and went 'pssst' and it didn't budge."

HEADS UP…

Little Johnny approaches Miss Jones' desk during homeroom and timidly says, "I don't wanna scare you or anything, but my Daddy says if I don't get better grades soon, somebody's gonna get a spanking."

BACKSEAT DRIVER…

Sheriff Robertson pulls Little Johnny's father over for speeding and begins, "I clocked you at over eighty miles per hour," says the sheriff.

Little Johnny's father replies, "Gee sheriff, I had my cruise control set at sixty."

"Don't be silly Dad," adds Little Johnny from the back seat, "This car doesn't have cruise control."

As the sheriff looks back at Little Johnny, he says sternly, "You know you're Dad's not wearing his seatbelt either."

Frantic at this point, Little Johnny's father says, "I only took it off so I could get my license out of my back pocket."

"Dad, since when do you wear your seatbelt?" adds Little Johnny.

As the sheriff continues writing out tickets, Little Johnny's father turns around to the backseat and yells, "Would you please shut up?"

The sheriff looks to the backseat and asks, "Does your Dad always talk to you this way?"

"Only when he's been drinking," replies Little Johnny.

GOAT...

Little Johnny's parents invite Father Harrison over for dinner one Friday evening. While his parents get things ready in the kitchen, Little Johnny and Father Harrison go ahead and have a seat in the dining room.

Curious by now, Father Harrison asks, "Do you know what we're having for dinner?"

Little Johnny replies, "I believe we're having goat."

"Are you sure about that?"

"I'm pretty sure. Just the other day, I overheard my parents say that Friday was as good a time as any to have the old goat for dinner."

LEARNER'S PERMIT...

Having just gotten his learner's permit, Little Johnny decides to see what his Dad's car has underneath the hood. Unfortunately, at the top of the next hill, Sheriff Robertson is waiting on him and before Little Johnny can slow down, the blue lights come on. Reluctantly, Little Johnny pulls over to the shoulder and rolls down his window. As Sheriff Robertson approaches the car, he sarcastically says, "I've been waiting for you all day."

While holding out his license, Little Johnny replies, "Yeah, well I got here as fast as I could."

ALL TUCKED IN...

One summer evening during a violent thunderstorm, Little Johnny is being tucked in by his mother. Just as she's about to turn the lights off, Little Johnny asks, "Mommy, will you sleep with me tonight?"

"I can't dear," she says, "I have to sleep with Daddy."

After a short silence, Little Johnny says, "Daddy's a big sissy too... huh?"

EASTER DRESS...

Lanie and Little Johnny are sitting next to each other in church. Following the service, Father Harrison stops by both of them and notices Lanie's new dress, "What a beautiful Easter dress you have on Lanie. Is it new?"

"Yes sir," replies Lanie.

Feeling left out, Little Johnny adds, "And her Mom says it's a real bitch to iron!"

HEAD COUNT...

At the breakfast table one morning, Little Johnny asks, "Mommy, why does Daddy have so few hairs on top of his head?"

"He thinks a lot," replies his mother.

"Why do you have so many?"

CHEERS...

On a dare, Little Johnny sneaks into the local tavern. He then proceeds to walk up to the first waitress he sees and hollers out, "Get me a beer."

The waitress eyeballs him for a moment and replies back to him, "Look, do you really want to get me in trouble?"

"Maybe later, but right now I want a beer."

BALCONY...

To get some alone time, Little Johnny's parents tell him he is a secret agent and his mission is to go out onto the balcony to see if any of the neighbors are up to no good.

After a half hour or so, Little Johnny comes back inside and reports on the neighbor's activities, "It looks like the Harrisons got a new SUV...Old Man Taylor is talking to his plants again... and I'm pretty sure the Robertsons are having sex."

"What in the world makes you think the Robertsons are having sex?"

"Well, their son was standing out on the balcony too."

SOUR MILK...

During Home Economics class, Miss Jones makes sure to stand by the refrigerator before asking her next question. "Little Johnny, do you know what helps keep milk from turning sour?"

"Why, of course...keep it in the cow!"

THE FOUR SEASONS...

Hoping to give him some confidence by asking an easy question, Miss Jones asks Little Johnny, "Can you name the four seasons?"

"Why, that's easy...cinnamon, pepper, nutmeg and garlic."

SICK DAY...

Little Johnny decides to call in sick to work. Since it's his last day at the car wash before school starts back up, he figures the repercussions will be minimal. His boss answers the phone on the third ring and Little Johnny says, "Boss, I'm very sorry but I won't be able to make it in to work today...my doctor says I have an acute case of anal glaucoma."

"What exactly is that?" asks his boss.

"I just can't see my ass coming to work today!"

WHAT'S IN A NAME?

While at the fall dance, Little Johnny decides to introduce himself to the new girl in school. He approaches her and asks her name.

"Carmen," she replies.

Trying to sustain the conversation, Little Johnny adds, "I've always thought Carmen was a pretty name."

"Yeah, my Mom always tells me that I was named after her two favorite things...cars and men. Well, enough about me, what's your name?"

"Golftits."

SAGE ADVICE...

While sitting on the front porch with his Uncle J.R. one afternoon, Little Johnny is bracing himself for the crown jewel of advice.

"If you only do one thing in life," says Uncle J.R., "make sure you marry a woman with small hands."

"And why's that?"

"It makes your pecker look bigger."

A BETTER PLACE…

Little Johnny's mother has some bad news for him about his dog when he arrives home from school. "Little Johnny, I'm so sorry, but Freckles was run over and killed earlier this afternoon. And I want you to know she is with God now."

Little Johnny thinks about this for a moment and asks, "What's God gonna do with a dead dog?"

SINK…

Due to their power being cut off, Little Johnny's family is forced to spend the night at the local motel. While hanging out in the motel lobby, Little Johnny hears the phone ring. As he walks over to the phone, the girl behind the counter says, "Go ahead, answer it…I've got my hands full with these boxes anyway."

Little Johnny hesitantly picks up the phone and says, "Hello."

The voice on the other side angrily says, "I've gotta leak in my sink!"

To which Little Johnny replies, "Go ahead."

GRAMMAR POLICE…

Following soccer practice, Little Johnny stands in line at the concession stand. Trying to make small talk, Little Johnny asks the girl in front of him, "So which team do you play for?"

"Don't you know better than to use a preposition at the end of a sentence?" replies the girl.

"So, which team do you play for...bitch?"

PROMISES, PROMISES...

Obviously disappointed in Little Johnny, Miss Jones says, "Didn't you promise me yesterday that you would start behaving?"

"Yes ma'am," answers Little Johnny.

"And didn't I promise to punish you if you didn't behave?"

"Yes ma'am, but since I broke my promise...I was hoping you'd break yours."

AND THEY'RE OFF...

It took some doing, but Little Johnny's mother finally talked her husband into taking their son to the zoo one Saturday. Later that night, Little Johnny's mother asks, "So how was the zoo?"

"Great," Little Johnny replies.

"And did your father have a good time?"

"He sure did...especially when one of the horses came in at 30 to 1!"

BASS ACKWARDS...

While waiting in the doctor's office, Little Johnny asks the man sitting next to him, "Why do you have your collar on backwards?"

The man, who was a priest, says "I'm a father."

"Well, my Daddy doesn't wear his collar like that."

"I am the father of many."

"How many? Because my Daddy has two boys and a girl, and I've never seen him wear his collar backwards."

"I am the father of hundreds."

"If that's the case, maybe you should wear your pants backwards instead of your collar."

HAPPY DAYS...

While sitting at a picnic table during their family reunion, Little Johnny asks, "Why is Aunt J.J. so drunk?"

Somewhat hesitant to answer, his Mom says, "Well son, Aunt J.J. has been like that ever since she and Uncle J.R. split up earlier this year."

"Wow, you wouldn't think a person could celebrate that long."

HI HO…

While visiting the horse track with his father, Little Johnny spots one of the jockeys sitting at a nearby table and figures it would be neat to get an autograph. Although a little put off by the request, the jockey quickly signs Little Johnny's race program. During the exchange, Little Johnny accidentally spills his soft drink all over the jockey's lap.

"I am not happy!" says the jockey.

"Oh yeah…well which one of the seven dwarfs are you?"

CROCODILE…

During their weekly spelling bee, Miss Jones asks, "Little Johnny, how do you spell crocodile?"

Little Johnny awkwardly begins, "k-r-o-c-k-a-d-i-l-e."

"That's incorrect."

"It may be incorrect…but you asked me how I spell it."

STATING THE OBVIOUS…

Following a brief film in Science class one afternoon, Miss Jones asks, "Can anyone tell me the best way to prevent diseases caused by biting insects?"

"Don't bite any!" answers Little Johnny.

A TENSE SITUATION...

This year's English class has been really taxing on Miss Jones. Most of her class just can't seem to grasp what verb tense to use. Therefore, when it comes time for their weekly oral exam, Miss Jones has little confidence that today's results will be any better. Her first question is for Little Johnny, "Can you give me a sentence starting with I?"

"Sure," replies Little Johnny, "I is..."

Before he can even finish his sentence, Miss Jones interrupts, "Will you never learn? Always say I am!"

"Okay...I am the ninth letter of the alphabet."

DEAR SANTA...

To help Little Johnny get into the spirit of Christmas, his parents think it would be a good idea for him to help answer some of the younger children's letters to Santa Clause. As he thumbs through some of the letters, Little Johnny comes across one that reads, "Dear Santa, I've been very good this year and all I really want for you to send me this Christmas is a baby brother. Sincerely, Lanie."

"Not quite feeling the holiday cheer, Little Johnny writes back, "Dear Lanie, Send me your mother and I'll see what I can do for you."

LIE LIKE A DOG...

After reading over Little Johnny's essay about his dog Freckles, Miss Jones suspiciously inquires, "This essay of yours sure is similar to the one your sister wrote this time last year?"

"I can see how you might think that," replies Little Johnny, "Since we do have the same dog and all."

WEIRD SCIENCE...

Although Science class is really starting to frustrate Little Johnny, Miss Jones finally asks him a question he remembers the answer to, "What is the chemical formula for water?"

Little Johnny proudly answers, "h-i-j-k-l-m-n-o!"

"Where on earth did you come up with an answer like that?"

"Yesterday, did you not say it was H to O?"

G.W....

Hoping to drive home to her class the importance of honesty, Miss Jones finishes up the story of George Washington and the cherry tree, "Not only did George Washington chop down his father's cherry tree, he admitted to doing so. With that being said, can anyone tell me why his father didn't punish him?"

Little Johnny smugly answers, "Because George still had the axe in his hand?"

SAVING GRACE...

Little Johnny's parents invite Father Harrison over for dinner one evening. While his parents are in the kitchen preparing the meal, Little Johnny and Father Harrison are left sitting at the dinner table. In an effort to break the awkward silence Father Harrison asks, "So, does your family say a prayer before dinner?"

"Not usually," answers Little Johnny, "Mom's a pretty good cook."

YOU'RE NEXT...

Little Johnny and his friend Tim try to make the best of a wedding they are forced to attend. Obviously frustrated by something, Tim finally speaks up, "Don't you just get tired of all the old people coming up to you at weddings, poking you in the ribs and saying, you're next...you're next?"

"I used to," replies Little Johnny, "but they've quit doing that to me ever since I started doing the same thing to them at funerals."

EAR ACHE...

Little Johnny strolls into Dr. Swinney's waiting area, approaches the receptionist and says, "There's something wrong with my dick."

The receptionist proceeds to scold Little Johnny, "How dare you say something like that in front of all these patients. Why can't you just say there's something wrong with your ear or something? And save the sordid details for Dr. Swinney."

Having given it some thought, Little Johnny clears his throat and says, "There's something wrong with my ear."

Thinking she's gotten through to this young man, the receptionist smiles and asks, "Exactly what's wrong with your ear?"

"I can't piss out of it."

DRINK OF WATER…

Five minutes after being tucked in bed, Little Johnny yells, "Dad, I'm thirsty. Can you bring me a drink of water?"

"No, you had your chance," replies his father.

Little Johnny asks again, "Dad, can I please have a drink of water?"

"I told you no…and if you ask one more time, I'm coming in there and giving you a butt-whippin'!"

"Dad, when you come give me my butt-whippin', could you bring a drink of water?"

SKINNY-DIPPIN'…

Aunt J.J. asks Little Johnny to grab a bucket and pick her some peaches for her famous cobbler. Little Johnny remembers that Uncle J.R. planted several peach trees down by the pond a few years back, so he knows exactly where to go.

As he nears the pond, Little Johnny hears giggling and as he gets even closer he notices several young ladies skinny-dipping in his uncle's pond. Well, it doesn't take long for the ladies to spot Little Johnny and one of them shouts, "You'll never see us naked…'cause we're not coming out until you leave!"

Little Johnny holds up his bucket and says, "Oh, I'm not here to watch you ladies swim around naked…I'm here to feed the alligator."

BOYS WILL BE BOYS…

Little Johnny comes home from school one afternoon with a black eye. As soon as his father sees it he says, "Little Johnny, how many times do I have to tell you not to fight with your classmates?"

"But Daddy," Little Johnny explains, "It wasn't my fault. This morning in homeroom…when we all stood up to say our prayers, I noticed that Miss Jones' dress was hung up in the crack of her butt. Well, I simply reached over and pulled it out for her. That's when she socked me!"

"Little Johnny," says his father, "Women just don't appreciate little boys doing that sort of thing. Do you understand?"

"Yes sir," Little Johnny whimpers.

Sure enough, the very next day, Little Johnny comes home with another black eye. "I thought we understood each other, son," his father says. "What on earth happened this time?"

"But Daddy," Little Johnny explains, "It wasn't my fault. This morning in homeroom…when we all stood up to say our prayers…I noticed that Miss Jones' dress was once again hung up in the crack of her butt. Billy, who sits right next to me, reached over and pulled it out. Well, I remembered what you told me… that women just don't appreciate little boys doing that sort of thing…so I nudged it back in for her!"

SHEER POETRY…

Little Johnny hurries to the podium to recite his poem…after all, he spent the entire weekend perfecting it.

> "Mary had a little lamb
> Her father shot it dead
> Now it goes to school with her
> Between two hunks of bread."

DISORIENTED…

During class, Miss Jones asks, "Little Johnny, I'd like for you to use the word disoriented in a sentence for me."

Little Johnny answers, "If you take an Oriental person and spin them around several times, they may become disoriented."

BAD LUCK…

After falling out of his tree house, Little Johnny slips in and out of a coma for several days. When he finally comes to, he motions for his mother to come closer as he holds back the tears, "Mommy, you've always been there for me. You were there when I wrecked my scooter. You were there when I broke my kneecap playing soccer. You were even there when I got my first cavity. And now…here you are by my side once again. You know what?"

Full of emotion his Mom answers, "What dear?"

"I'm beginning to think you're bad luck."

COMPLIMENT…

All ready for church, Little Johnny hops on his Mom's bed to watch cartoons while his mother continues to get ready. As she looks into her full-length mirror, she says, "I look horrible…I feel fat…and ugly. Pay me a compliment."

Little Johnny replies, "Your eyesight's 20/20."

AND HOLDING…

Little Johnny asks, "Aunt J.J, exactly how old are you?"

"Thirty nine and holding," his aunt answers.

"And how old would you be if you let go?"

FORGIVENESS...

Hoping the children have learned something following his Sunday school lesson, Father Harrison asks them, "What must we as Christians do before we can expect forgiveness from God?"

"Sin!" answers Little Johnny.

HARSH REQUIREMENTS...

Curious as to what the answer will be, Father Harrison asks a very general question during his Sunday school class, "Where do you want to go?"

"Heaven!" Lanie cries out.

"And what do you have to be to get there?" asks Father Harrison.

"Dead!" answers Little Johnny.

ANIMAL CRACKERS...

As Little Johnny and his mother put away the groceries, Little Johnny suddenly empties an entire box of animal crackers on the kitchen table.

"What do you think you're doing?" asks his mother.

"The box says don't eat if seal broken," answers Little Johnny, "so I'm looking for the seal."

THEORY & REALITY...

One evening, Little Johnny shows his father a homework assignment and asks, "Daddy, could you explain to me the difference between theory and reality?"

His Dad tells him, "Go to your Mom and ask her if she would sleep with another man for a million dollars."

Little Johnny does as he is told. "Well yes, I suppose I would," answers his mother.

His Dad then tells him, "Now go ask your sis if she would sleep with a man for a million dollars."

Little Johnny once again does as he is told. "Yes, I suppose I would," she answers.

"Son," his father explains, "you should now have a clear understanding of the difference between theory and reality. In theory...we're sitting on two million dollars. In reality...we're living with a couple of whores."

T.G.I.F....

One Friday morning in homeroom, Lanie asks Little Johnny, "How do you like my new T.G.I.F. shirt?"

"Very nice", answers Little Johnny.

Thinking she can stump Little Johnny in front of the entire class Lanie continues, "Do you even know what T.G.I.F. stands for?"

"Tits go in front?"

A LADY NEVER TELLS...

One afternoon, Little Johnny's aunt stops by for a visit. "How old are you Aunt J.J.?" asks Little Johnny.

"Well, that's not a question that you ask a lady," she says.

"How much do you weigh?" he asks.

"That is not a question you ask a lady," she says.

Little Johnny is persistent, "Aunt J.J., why don't you and Uncle J.R. sleep in the same bed?"

"That's enough! These are not questions you ask a lady! Go to your room!"

On his way, Little Johnny trips over his aunt's purse. As he picks it up, her driver's license falls out. Little Johnny carefully looks it over and rejoins his aunt in the family room.

"I know how old you are," states Little Johnny confidently.

"And how do you know that?" she replies.

"I also know how much you weigh," adds Little Johnny.

"And how do you know that?" she once again replies.

Ignoring her questions, Little Johnny continues, "I also know why you and Uncle J.R. don't sleep in the same bed."

Frantic at this point, Aunt J.J. raises her voice, "Little Johnny, how do you know all this about me?"

"Well, I found your driver's license and it clearly says that you're 32 years old and that you weigh 135 pounds. It also explains why you and Uncle J.R. don't sleep in the same bed…you got an 'F' in sex!"

WHEEL OF MISFORTUNE…

One day, Little Johnny is sitting in class when Miss Jones announces that they are going to play a new game. She will choose a letter, and in turn, whomever she calls on will pick an animal that starts with that letter.

Miss Jones begins, "Ready? The first letter is 'C'." Several students raise their hands, but none higher than Little Johnny. Miss Jones thinks to herself that there are too many naughty words that began with the letter 'C' and that calling on Little Johnny would be inviting trouble. So she calls on Tim.

Tim stands up and says, "Cat."

"Very good Tim! The next letter is 'S'."

Little Johnny immediately raises his hand again, begging Miss Jones to call on him. Once again, there are just too many naughty words that begin with the letter 'S'. She calls on Amy instead.

Amy stands up and says, "Snake."

"Good answer! Next is the letter 'R'."

By this time, Little Johnny is jumping up and down in the aisle trying to get Miss Jones' attention. She thinks for a moment and can't think of anything naughty starting with the letter 'R'. She finally calls on Little Johnny.

Little Johnny says, "Rat...with a big pecker this long."

SINGLE...

Though usually a stock boy, the grocery store is short handed one afternoon so Little Johnny is stuck working one of the registers. One of his first customers has just about one of everything in her cart, which prompts Little Johnny to ask, "Single, are you?"

"Why yes...how'd you guess?"

"Because you're ugly."

THE TALES WE TELL...

For homework, Miss Jones instructs her students to think of a story and, in turn, conclude what the moral of that story is. The following day Miss Jones asks for volunteers to share their stories with the class.

Sherry raises her hand. "My Dad owns a farm and every Sunday we load the chicken eggs on his truck and drive into town so we can sell them at the market. Well, one Sunday we ran over a pothole and all of the eggs fell onto the road and cracked. The moral of my story is; don't keep all your eggs in one basket."

Next is Jarrod. "Well, my Dad owns a farm too and every weekend we take the chicken eggs and put them in an incubator. Last weekend only eight of the twelve eggs hatched.

The moral of my story is; don't count your chickens before they're hatched."

Last is Little Johnny. "My Uncle J.R. was a fighter pilot in Vietnam. One dark and stormy night his plane was shot down over enemy territory…narrowly escaping death, he leaped from his plane clutching only a fifth of whiskey, a machine gun and a large machete. Well, he had just finished off the whiskey when his parachute was ripped to shreds by enemy gunfire causing him to free-fall the remaining distance. At least fifty enemy soldiers surrounded him as he fell to the ground. With assassin-like precision, Uncle J.R. used his machine gun to drop one soldier after another. By the time he was out of ammunition, there were less than twenty soldiers remaining. That's when Uncle J.R. reached for his machete and was able to butcher over a dozen more. All of the soldiers that were still living at that point, he finished off with his bare hands.

Miss Jones is dumbfounded, "Could there possibly be a moral to this story?"

"Yeah…don't mess with Uncle J.R. when he's been drinking!"

GREAT LAKES…

During Geography class, Miss Jones asks if anyone can name each of the Great Lakes.

Little Johnny chimes in immediately, "Why would I need to name them…they've already been named!"

SCREW YOU...

Little Johnny and Lanie are peacefully sitting on the front porch when all of a sudden, Little Johnny shouts, "Screw you, Lanie!"

"Screw you, Little Johnny!" replies Lanie.

A moment or two later, Little Johnny again shouts, "Screw you, Lanie!"

And again Lanie replies, "Screw you, Little Johnny!"

After several minutes of this, Little Johnny's father sticks his head out the front door and asks, "What on earth are you kids doing?"

"We're having oral sex!" they reply in unison.

BENIGN...

During her lesson on health issues, Miss Jones asks, "Do any of you know what benign means?"

Little Johnny hollers, "Benign is what you are after you be eight!"

DECEPTIVELY DESCRIPTIVE...

One day Miss Jones brings a bag full of food to class and says, "I'm going to reach into this bag and describe a type of food. I then want one of you to guess what I'm describing. Okay, first… it's somewhat round and red in color."

Of course, Little Johnny raises his hand high, but Miss Jones wisely ignores him and picks Amy, who promptly answers, "An apple."

"No Amy, it's a beet, but I like your thinking. Now for the second…it's soft, fuzzy, and has a reddish-brown tint."

By this time, Little Johnny is noticeably irritated and blurts out, "Hey, I've got one for you Miss Jones…let me put my hand in my pocket. OK, I've got it…its round, hard, and has a head on it."

"Little Johnny!" she cries. "That's disgusting!"

"Nope," answers Little Johnny, "It's a quarter, but I like your thinking!"

BEAUTY SECRET…

Little Johnny curiously watches as his mother rubs cold cream onto her face.

"Why do you do that, Mommy?" Little Johnny asks.

"To make myself beautiful," she replies.

As his mother begins to remove the cream with a tissue, Little Johnny further inquires, "What's wrong Mommy, are you giving up?"

WOOSHIE!

Whether they knew it or not at the time, each of the following people helped contribute to this collection: Ali Thompson, Amy Nielsen, Bill Burns, Billy Fant, Bill Panas, Bobby McCurry, Bill "Boot" Fant, Brad Whitehead, Brad Wood, Charles Hipp, Cindy Wiley, Cole Rawden, Craig Rawden, Garnett Stancil, Greg Adams, James Hillard, James Ricco, Jamie Youngblood, Jason Fant, Jean Bowick, Jeremy Khars, Jim Sims, Joan Clark, Joey Stamba, John House, Kevin Cissell, Leo Miller, Marcus West, Mark Owens, Mary Virginia Gardner, Matt Beagle, Melanie Laird, Missy Atkisson, Peter Magargee, Philip Rountree, Roy Swift, Scott Travis and Wade Stanton.

The cover was a collaborative effort as well: cover boy (Davis Fant), cover photographer (Elizabeth DeRamus – check out her work at www.elizabethderamus.com) and cover designer (Elise Page).

While in a more latent fashion, the following people also helped mold the overall mood of this collection: my mom for playing those Richard Pryor records during her pregnancy with me, my dad for encouraging me to stay up past my bedtime as a toddler to catch up on reruns of *The Benny Hill Show*, and most of all my adoring wife for laughing with me and not at me.